Faster, Better Decision-Making

Faster, Better Decision-Making

Faster, Better Decision-Making

How to Make Good Decisions Quickly in Your Daily Life

Debra Morrison & Instafo

instafo

Copyright © Instafo

All rights reserved.

It is impermissible to reproduce any part of this book without prior consent. All violations will be prosecuted to the fullest extent of the law.

While attempts have been made to verify the information contained within this publication, neither the author nor the publisher assumes any responsibility for errors, omissions, interpretation or usage of the subject matter herein.

This publication contains the opinions and ideas of its author and is intended for informational purpose only. The author and publisher shall in no event be held liable for any loss or other damages incurred from the usage of this publication.

ISBN 978-1-540-69277-1

Printed in the United States of America

First Edition

CONTENTS

Chapter 1: Inner-Workings of Decision-Making

1.1 Decisions that Personally Define You..................6

1.2 Behind the Curtain of Choices......................8

Chapter 2: Assembly Line of Decision-Making

2.1 Not So Random..12

2.2 Formulistic Approach..................................14

2.3 Systemize Your Process...............................16

Chapter 3: 50 Shades of Decision-Making

3.1 Not So Black and White After All................20

3.2 Rules of the Game......................................21

3.3 Beat the Dreaded Decider's Block..............26

Chapter 4: Anatomy of Decision-Making

4.1 A Tripod to Support Better Decisions........28

4.2 Awareness of Options................................29

4.3 Preparedness of Actions............................33

4.4 Evaluation of Consequences..37

Chapter 5: Elimination Process of Decision-Making
5.1 Eliminate Enemy Called 'Regret'..............................41
5.2 Battle Plan..43
5.3 Attack!...45
5.4 Accept Victory...47

Chapter 6: Finalization of Decision-Making
6.1 A Matter of Choice...49
6.2 Decide Responsibly..50

Faster, Better Decision-Making

Faster, Better Decision-Making

Chapter 1:
Inner-Workings of Decision-Making

Decisions that Personally Define You

Decisions, decisions…life wouldn't be complete without them. They make our days more entertaining, sometimes frustrating, and definitely a whole lot more complex.

Have you found yourself saying, "*What should I do?*" one too many times? From "*because I want to*" to "*it's my* life" to "*I had no choice,*" life is full of not only decisions, but also justifications for why we make those decisions.

Decisions can hit you at 200mph in your face, or they can creep up on you as habits. You may find yourself making conscious or automatic decisions, opinions, or changes on a daily basis. You probably don't even realize it – decisions are EVERYWHERE. (Beyoncé might have told us that girls run the world, but it's actually our *decisions* that do.)

Decisions are like breathing – you don't realize you are doing it until it becomes hard to do. Ironically, they are both critical for life to move forward effectively.

Sometimes, decisions are straightforward, much like a cause-and-effect relationship. For example, at work, processes and objectives are defined clearly. The decisions you make align within those boundaries.

- To learn about professional decision-making, you can easily access about seven gazillion other research papers and resources out there, published by eminent authorities, which talk about just that. There is a wealth of information in the world, detailing different professional avenues and delving far beyond the scope of what you'll get here. Therefore, this will NOT be about the science of professional decision-making. Instead, our <u>main focus</u> is unraveling the mystery of **personal decision-making**, meaning the decisions that run our lives...actually, the decisions *we make* that run our lives.

So, let's enter into an alternate universe in which we FULLY understand what it takes to make the best decisions possible, and then those decisions pan out EXACTLY as we plan! In this universe, of course, pigs fly, money grows on trees, and you're married to Angelina Jolie or Brad Pitt.

Behind the Curtain of Choices

Alas, Angelina is taken. And much like she is married to Brad, our decisions are married (happily or unhappily) to **emotions**.

Every time you decide something, you are indulging in one or more sacred emotion of security, love, happiness, strength, righteousness, etc. Even when decisions are based on logic and intelligence, they still hold emotion. Decisions carry weight. They either add to the greater good of the individual and/or humanity or, sadly, the demise.

This is why we are not able to so easily flip a coin to make every decision of our lives, although wouldn't that make life so much easier. :)

At this point, if you're not convinced about the notion that emotions are at the heart of our every decision, then it is time for a lesson on the evolution of human mind (the CliffsNotes version, of course).

Physician and neuroscientist Paul D. MacLean created the Triune brain model, which focuses on, you guessed it, the brain. It shows that the limbic system (seat of instincts and emotions) was actually established in the brain much earlier than the neocortex system (seat for logic, reasoning and rationale). We may never know if the chicken came before the egg, but it does seem that emotions did come before reasoning. This means that (drum roll...) the most "logical" decision *can* be traced back to a very basic instinct or emotion.

Because decisions are so enmeshed with deeply personal emotions, people are often unable to relate to *others'* reasoning of decisions and actions.

For example, you might decide to have children at an early age because you always dreamed of being a mom or dad. Your friend might choose to not have children at all because he or she had a terrible upbringing. Decisions related to culture, parenting, lifestyle, patriotism, religion, politics, and so on, can all be traced back to personal emotion. Because you might have a different emotion than your friend related to a decision, conflict can arise. It is your part to be aware of what this conflict stems from, and be cognizant that those around you may "decision-make" differently than you.

So if you are here reading this, you're probably at the cusp of a seemingly important decision. You are probably wondering if you're going to make the *right* decision or not. Should you flip a coin? How about, instead, you start to ask yourself this: *"What emotion is connected with this decision?"*

After all, it's not the decision you're anxious about…it's the *consequences* of that decision.

Chapter 2:

Assembly Line of Decision-Making

Not So Random

There are days when you're so overwhelmed with the multiple events or issues coming your way that you can barely see straight. It might be a crazy day at work meeting deadlines (or not, as we can all relate to), or it could be trying to put your three kids down for a nap. You are exhausted, your attention span is at a scary minimum, and it would be a miracle if you could even decide what to eat for dinner.

Many of us lead very busy lives. The days are flying by faster than you could even *say* the words, *"I know exactly what I am doing."*

In these times, you need to stop and reflect. Can you make the right decisions fast enough to match your pace of life, or will you be left floundering behind? How can YOU master **decision-making**?

Before trying to tackle important, life-changing decisions that need *time* and *brain power*, let's cross a hurdle of small decisions that do not need significant thought. We're talking about the stuff that impacts your life minimally. This part is tricky because you have to look at these decisions as being *split up* into **goals** and **tasks**. Let's explain...

- For example, it's a decision to work out every day and choose healthy food options. This is a long-term goal you are setting for yourself. The tasks associated with this are deciding what kind of exercise or food option you're going to pick each day.

The <u>Law of Diminishing Returns</u> suggests that, at some point, the effort you're putting towards a certain result becomes *more than* the value of the outcome.

Using the example above, if you spend too much time wondering what exercise to do or staring inside your fridge confused on what to eat, your results are not going to get any better. It's like you purchased tickets to the game, but never quite made it there.

Within this context, you can *decide* a <u>pattern in advance</u> and **optimize your efforts** towards following through and executing the decision.

Formulistic Approach

Building predictability helps curb situations where you are in a panic and, in turn, choose hastily and perhaps even irrationally. This means you can stop yourself from freaking out over every little decision. Just apply the Law of Diminishing Returns to the decision-making that falls into your routine on a daily basis; it will go one of two ways:

1. **Pre-decide** – Many decisions can be made ahead of time and sometimes in bulk (the Costco of decision-making, if you will). For example, take that dreadful decision you might make every day: what to wear for work. Ladies (or men – not here to judge), don't panic. Instead, on Sundays, look in your closet and don't grab just one outfit for the next day; go ahead and plan your outfits for the entire week. The inertia will actually enable you to decide faster. Plus, instead of having to repeatedly stress every morning about what you're going to wear, you got it done in one chunk of time! The same goes for planning your (or the family's) meals for the week, creating a shopping list for an upcoming season sale, or drawing out specifics of your weekly workout. Use timetables or schedules to map out your week, build predictability, and maximize your time

management. (*Psst*...management gurus call this "planning.")

2. **Automate** – Once you start to pre-decide, you can further optimize your time by using "smart" machines (i.e. cell phones, computers, iPads, Apple watches, or whatever other cool stuff you have these days). If possible, use the "smart" calendars built in to manage your time. For example, if you've decided on a meal and workout plan for the week, use the calendar to block time to shop, cook, exercise and remind you of any other activities. Set reminders to help you stay on track. Optimize the use of machines, and use them as virtual assistants.

Systemize Your Process

Let's now put the focus on YOU, specifically. What are *your* daily decisions that take up more time than you feel is necessary? These things are important **only to you** and it doesn't have an effect on others in your life.

Go ahead and list three things that you can pre-decide and automate. Preferably choose things that are repetitive and time-consuming.

Examples:

a. Fitness – Create weekly schedules and meal plans to reduce your daily stress about what to cook.

b. Fashion – Spend a chunk of time on Sunday to plan and organize your work-wear during the week.

c. Finances – Set up online banking on your phone to manage basic banking when you're waiting in line for your coffee…or lying in bed trying to pretend it's not Monday morning.

d. Errands – Spend a block of time scheduling repetitive tasks and reminders in advance on your "smart" calendar (i.e. wellness check-ups, dentist visits, home maintenance, etc.)

e. Bills – Automate your monthly payments with auto-pay, which is a luxury almost every business that hasn't lived under a rock for the past ten years has set up.

f. Organization – Use productivity apps like Cozi, SuperNotes, Paper by Fifty Three, Asana, or OneNote as both your personal and professional dashboards.

g. Shopping – When shopping, use a list. Save money, time, impulse behavior, and regret.

h. Chores – If you can, outsource/delegate chores to your kids, kids in the neighborhood who want to earn pocket money, or even professionals. This includes cleaning, mowing the lawn, laundry, and anything else that is monotonous. This will free you up to take care of other important matters.

i. Driving – Reduce driving and carpool, taxi, Uber, Lyft, or use public transport. Utilize that time you *would* be driving to work on an assignment, read the book you keep meaning to get to, or call your grandmother. Simply put, be productive.

Chapter 3:

50 Shades of Decision-Making

Not So Black and White After All

Ever been in a situation where you order something at a restaurant and then get tempted with another person's order afterwards? More than a few times, maybe? It's fine – it is only human to make decisions that you regret later on. As they say, hindsight is always 20/20.

Too much of our time is spent worrying about the **consequences of our decisions** and nurturing **anxiety about the options we didn't select**.

Yes, when we *do* make decisions, there is some amount of relief that we FINALLY DID IT. However, that anxiousness we have from the finality of it all does take away from the effectiveness of that decision. Believe it or not, there are plenty of ways you are sabotaging your own decision-making.

Rules of the Game

If you want to stop wasting your time and effort and start making successful, straightforward decisions, then read on.

Take these steps to help you snap out of these self-destructive behaviors:

> 1. **Evaluate *right* vs. *wrong* decisions** – Assess decisions on the basis of their workability…being able to tell right from wrong means these decisions should, of course, be subjective, but will have limited flexibility and conflict. Decide: are the consequences attached to

this decision **workable** or **not workable** in the context of your goals and/or emotions?

2. **Don't procrastinate** – Not making timely decisions only gives you less time and less power to be effective. Nobody enjoys tolerating a procrastinator. It's ironic that most people delay decisions because they don't want to deal with consequences, when those consequences are inevitable no matter what! You might as well take the plunge and at least be the one in control.

3. **Don't do it because others are doing it** – Don't jump off a bridge just because your friend is doing it (DUH). Use your own judgment in a situation and assess your options. *Getting influenced is not the basis for a well-informed decision.* Given a situation, two people may make opposing decisions for their own reasons (remember the example from before – everyone has their own subjective emotions that influence their decisions). YOU are liable for your own actions. Don't ever blindly follow the "herd."

4. Ask questions about options and consequences – On what basis are you making that decision? If you do not have enough information, you end up shooting in the dark and probably shooting yourself in the foot. When faced with issues where a decision is imminent, drop the assumptions and build your information pool. "Hoping for the best" is an attitude, not an approach.

5. **Choose only your way** – This one links to the above point. Every decision is different and requires uncovering relevant information before making up your mind. Sometimes, we put the cart before the horse and assume that we know best…especially when it comes to *deciding* for other people. Speak for yourself, and let others do the same.

6. **Reflect** – Analysis paralysis? Choice overload? Decisions can be scary! The uncertainty of results or the consequences of those results loom over you like a ghost in the night. If you can't stop thinking about all the

things that *could* go wrong, you are just at the point where you can't sign on the dotted line. It's time to reboot. Plug yourself back into your goals, emotions, and values. Then, evaluate your options. If fear is holding you back, the results will be terrifying. Get over it, and make that jump.

7. **Don't choose one way because of a past decision** – *"Because last time I did this, this time I'll do this"*…sound familiar? This is NOT a strong foundation for decision-making. This is a different version of the coin toss. Don't choose "heads" because last time you chose "tails." It could very well be "heads" again. At the risk of sounding like a broken record, **every decision is different.** Collect your information, evaluate all options, understand the consequences, and then make your decision.

8. **Don't let others influence you** – Smell fear in this one too? Oftentimes, we find ourselves in an internal conflict – you want to choose option A but think that

option B is more socially appropriate or expected. Circle back to understanding workability and the emotional need that your decision is riding on, and then decide. Your choice may not please everyone, but it is the best for you at the time, and that's what matters.

9. **Focus on emotion over logic** – Unless you're doing a math or science problem, every decision you make will have elements of both logic and emotion in it. Try raising a child or managing a relationship with only one element and you'll know what that's like. You tell your child he or she is not allowed to drink underage, because it's the law. But the emotion of *being scared of what could happen* to your child under the influence is what drives that decision. Collecting information before making a decision is both a logical and creative process; so is evaluating it. However, when a decision appeals to your emotions positively, that is when you're ready to move forward. Basically, if you have that gut feeling, listen to it.

10. **Don't be wishy-washy** – Have you ever decided something, and then changed your mind later on? Of course you have! Who hasn't?! Once in a while is fine, but to make a habit out of it will seriously cripple your confidence and effectiveness during decision-making. Be thorough with your homework, and take the time to understand the consequences. After that, make the decision and don't second-guess yourself.

Beat the Dreaded Decider's Block

Let's focus on areas where you are stuck and unable to make decisions. It could be regarding your education, relationship, career, investments, health, or anything else.

Pick two areas and write down all the reasons why you are not able to make a decision.

a. What's stopping you? What are your fears?

b. What are the (negative) feelings about this decision or consequences?

c. Have you discussed this decision with other relevant people you trust? Have you considered recommendations and best practices?

d. Are there blanks (uncertainties) you can fill in with more research?

e. Have you looked into your biases and assumptions for this issue?

Now that you've started to perform an autopsy on the barriers blocking you, zone in on the ten areas explained above and identify your stumbling block.

In the next segment, continue to weigh your decisions and options to move towards better decision-making.

Chapter 4:

Anatomy of Decision-Making

A Tripod to Support Better Decisions

So congratulations, you are at the point where you have decided to make a decision!

Decisions are precursor to action and *decision IS an action in itself*. Now, let's learn about the anatomy of a decision. No need to be timid – this will be quick and painless. :)

Keep two of your pending decisions close by and work on "closing the deal."

Let's keep it simple; decisions are a balance of three important aspects:

1. Awareness of options

2. Preparedness of actions

3. Evaluation of consequences

Awareness of Options

Tip: Understand, evaluate and generate cause & effect for each option.

Many are tempted to move quickly towards the action and execution of their decision without spending adequate time in this area. Imagine someone asked you to have lunch and laid out a buffet spread for you to choose from. Without exploring all the options, you eat only the first two dishes you lay your eyes on and leave.

Whenever you find yourself thinking about options *after* the entire decision has unfolded (and possibly regretting the current circumstances), that's a result of not having spent enough time understanding your options and related consequences.

This is a *rational* activity. Since your emotions may be running high, giving this stage the quality time and thought it deserves is crucial.

In the following situations, one may be able to think of various ideas to resolve the problem. While it's easy to say that people will deal with the same situation differently, it's a fact that your own responses may vary depending on your emotions and rationale.

Here are some examples:

- You're stressed because things have been rocky in your relationship and you two fought yet again.

What are your options in dealing with this stress or situation?

- Your mom is really sick and you want to go visit her and help out, but your job is extremely demanding. What will you do?

- You're totally convinced your professor hates you because no matter how hard you work, your grade is a C+ at best. You're ready to give up. What decision should you make?

List the various choices you have. Now, remove the inferior options immediately. You can then take the remaining options you have and stack them up against these questions:

- Do you understand what the decision entails? (List all of the reasons why it's important to make a decision in this situation. This will help maintain focus on what you want to achieve from the decision.)

- What are your choices? Are these your only choices? Why?

- What other options do you have besides these choices?

- Are your options at all impacted by your values or personal experiences?

- Will you need to make this decision again anytime in the future?

Sometimes, a person is able to explore options and figure out the next step just by some introspection. However, often, people find value in discussing their ideas with someone else, or by researching more information about the topic.

How you generate awareness of options is not as much based off your personal style, but more so on the nature of the decision. Different decisions require different approaches.

For example, if you have to make parenting decisions, it usually involves both parents. If you need to make decisions about picking a college or class, you'll need to do a lot of research on your own. If you are deciding what attitude changes you need to make in order to improve your eating habits, a lot of self-talk is necessary. You get the idea.

Preparedness of Actions

Tip: List and weigh the complexity involved with the actions taken subsequent to the decision.

If you look closely, decisions are our end goals, or the grand finale. Shedding weight or earning a college degree, becoming an entrepreneur or getting that black belt in karate – these are the outcomes of our primary decisions.

Now, repeat this mantra: **There is no decision without the doing.**

In other words, don't talk the talk if you can't walk the walk. Just deciding that you're going to lose weight doesn't give you results. You have to take actions consistent with the decision if you want the desired result.

Remember, the real story begins *after* you decide.

While working on generating awareness about the various options, you're obviously thinking about what needs to get done. It's possible that, in the past, you have made decisions just because they were *easy to do* or *the right thing*. This doesn't mean, though, that you've always gotten the results you wanted.

Whatever your justification may be for acting in a certain way, the bottom line is that **the execution of the decision is the most critical part of decision-making.**

Take the time and put in the effort needed to figure out what it takes for successful decision-making. You need to have all the clarity in the world to understand "The Plan" AND a "Plan B."

Notice the word **TIME** in this last paragraph. Both **timeline** AND **timeliness** are important elements in making an ultimate decision. (If you're still avoiding making that decision, refer back on procrastination and read it again. Don't set yourself up for failure.)

Ready to roll up your sleeves and get into action? Focus on your two pending decisions and ask yourself the following questions:

- What do you have to do *during* and *after* the decision?

- What emotions arise as you think about the actions involved?

- What can go wrong?

- Any cost benefit or ROI evaluation needed? (If yes, what are the possible outcomes?)

- Do you have the answers for the 5 Ws: who, what, when, where, why (and sometimes how)?

- Do you have a timeline?

- Will you need any help in executing this decision? How will you manage that?

A decision may take a second to make, but a year to execute. The (sometimes) loooong process is what constitutes action.

For example: Now that you've decided, you need to figure out the *actions* required to...

- Become an accountant

- Spend quality time with your family

- Improve your golf game

- Work on your relationship

- Grow your business

- Plan your next vacation

Evaluation of Consequences

<u>Tip</u>: Consequences of a decision are inevitable. Results and consequences are the "meat" in the decision-making sandwich.

Remember when we spoke about decisions being enmeshed with emotions? Well, all of the anticipation tied to decision-making does stem from emotion. You are unconsciously searching to find what will fulfill your emotional needs the most.

For example, you could be grappling with a situation similar to any of the following:

- "Going to college might help me get a decent job in the future, **BUT** getting a job right now will help me move out of my parents' house."

- "Should I ask for this promotion directly, **OR** just wait until the performance ratings are out?"

- "Should I buy the fully-loaded version of the car that looks sooooo sick, **OR** stay within my budget and buy something reasonably priced?"

Evaluate the consequences of the decision and your willingness to live with these consequences. Ask yourself this:

- What are the expected results?

- How does this decision impact me long-term?

- Will my rewards outweigh my efforts? (Reference the Law of Diminishing Returns.)

- Will I need to make this decision again anytime in the future?

- Any possibility of having regrets? What are they and how will I deal with them?

- How will this decision impact other decisions?

Are you getting tired of this dissection of your pending decision? You're almost there. The key here is to *communicate…with yourself*.

All of these questions may not apply to you, but through these questions you will create a platform to talk to yourself about *what you really want* and *how you plan to get it*.

Being confident about your decision also means being comfortable with the consequences of that decision.

Chapter 5:

Elimination Process of Decision-Making

Eliminate Enemy Called 'Regret'

Inherent to almost every decision is the element of **choice**. At a certain point in time, you made a decision, meaning you selected <u>one option</u> out of the few you had.

Evaluating a decision after its consequences have unfolded and realizing that other choices could have led to better results…well, that is the term we all know and hate: **regret**.

If decisions were strictly logical, regret wouldn't exist. But it does, so we can again go back and reiterate, *"Emotions are deeply enmeshed with decisions and their consequences."*

Regret is always a possible consequence of a decision. And if you'll excuse our French, "$hit happens." Not all decisions turn out to be your best move, and then regret is expected. However, regret from previous experiences *can* weigh on your future decisions.

While regret can be a very strong (and annoying) teacher, it can also become an enormous influencer. Depending on how significant the regret is, it may have enough power to alter your decision; it can make it become skewed, ineffective and destined for failure.

Every decision will have the potential to be highly effective, but can also nose-dive and leave you with regret. The evaluation of options and consequences is of prime importance for these reasons.

Let's face it – there are only two types of regrets: **regret over what happened** and **regret over what didn't happen.**

Whether you proposed or you should've, whether you gave it your best or didn't do enough, whether you didn't say it or shared too much, whether you acted immediately or waited too long, whether you followed your mind or your heart…whatever the scenario, the regret ensues because you should have done the opposite of the current situation.

Battle Plan

A few ways to minimize the *'potential of regret'* in a decision are:

1. **Discuss your decision with stakeholders and/or with people you trust.** This process can build your self-confidence when executing the decision.

2. **Be thorough in collecting relevant information.** This process can help control the uncertainties and enable you to learn more about the situation.

3. **Eliminate opinion – yours and others.'** Focusing on the facts and keeping the process objective will control the chaos, waste, and drama.

4. **Have a Plan B.** Unless your decision has an unbreakable scientific formula built in for accuracy, always prepare a back-up plan. Keeping your focus on the goal, while still having a Plan B (and maybe a Plan C), ensures that you continue moving towards your objective. This builds predictability (and gives you an escape route).

5. **Give it your best effort.** Many times the regret is just that you could've done better if you had worked harder (or smarter).

Dwelling on regret will NOT change your past decisions or alter the consequences that resulted.

What dwelling *does* do is hurt your self-confidence, faith, courage, risk-taking ability, appetite for rigor, and the chance to succeed.

And if all else fails and regret does take over, it's absolutely fine. We are only human. Grieve, learn from your mistakes, and move on. True, easier said than done, but that is a whole other conversation.

Attack!

Again, think about those two important pending decisions and ponder these questions:

- Do you have any previous regrets looming in your mind that are relevant to the pending decisions?

- Can you foresee any potential regrets for the pending decisions?

If *yes*, then this exercise is very important for you! Read this closely:

- What is the weakest point in your decision? How can you change that?

- Did you distinguish areas in your decision that you can control versus those you can't? Is your 'potential for regret' related to the former or the latter?

- What have you learned from the previous decisions you regret?

- How can you apply that learning in the context of the current decisions?

- Is what you learned productive or counter-productive for the pending decisions?

Think creatively to outwit your potential regret.

If you haven't realized it by now, we're essentially working backwards to help us make the right decision. We're doing this by steering away from the pain of regret as much as possible through understanding and anticipating its possible occurrence.

Accept Victory

Once you have arrived at your final decision, stay with it for a while. Let it soak in. Go for a run, sleep on it, have a drink – whatever gives you some relaxed "me-time" to chew on the decision.

Let your logic and intuition align before you take the next step.

This reflection time will give your emotions a chance to catch up and, in some cases, act up. Positive emotions help in generating more ideas to execute the decision. They create good hormones (adrenaline, endorphins) that are necessary for you to move ahead full steam.

Now that you're ready to move ahead, execute with confidence! A decision is only as good as its execution. Don't drop the ball.

As you move, one step at a time, tune in to the overall objectives and keep your eye on the prize.

If you continually evaluate and learn during the process, you're already on the winning track.

Chapter 6:

Finalization of Decision-Making

A Matter of Choice

Whether you're choosing your career or what to have for breakfast, it's *your* life.

The essence of every decision is to help you be a happy, successful, growing person. You always have the option to change your mind or make a different choice.

You will experience making bad decisions and, once in a while, even screw up royally. That's life and it is perfectly OK.

Many of the big decisions we are faced with are like school exams – to succeed, you can't wait until the last day to study; you work the whole semester to prepare for the exam.

Your experiences, attitudes, values and life goals all play a role in your decision-making. Whenever you get stuck in your decision, revisit your chapters and find the block that's holding you back.

Decide Responsibly

No matter what the decision, the only thing more important than the decision itself is *having responsibility*. You must own the decision, the process, the actions, and the consequences. Many leaders fail when they make decisions because they don't take responsibility for them.

Individual and group decisions have changed the course of history many times; decisions matter.

Remember that it's OK to take the time you need to make a strong decision. That, or you can leave it up to fate…coin toss, anyone??

Your decision…

Faster, Better Decision-Making

Made in the USA
Lexington, KY
17 December 2016